Cylinders

BY NANCY FURSTINGER

The Child's World

Published by The Child's World®
1980 Lookout Drive • Mankato, MN 56003-1705
800-599-READ • www.childsworld.com

Acknowledgments
The Child's World®: Mary Berendes, Publishing Director
Red Line Editorial: Editorial direction
The Design Lab: Design

Photographs ©: Anton Prado/Shutterstock Images,
cover (top left), 1 (top left), 3 (right), 5; Magnum
Johansson/Shutterstock Images, cover (top right),
1 (top right), 3 (left), 9; Shutterstock Images, cover
(bottom left), 1 (bottom left), 6, 11, 15, 17, 20, 23;
iStockphoto/Thinkstock, cover (bottom right),
1 (bottom right), 16, 21; JupiterImages/Creatas Images/
Thinkstock, 4; Valestock/Shutterstock Images, 10;
Dmitry Kalinovsky/Shutterstock Images, 12; Comstock/
Thinkstock, 13; Patrick Foto/Shutterstock Images, 18

ISBN: 9781623239831
LCCN: 2013947242

Printed in the United States of America
Mankato, MN
November, 2013
PA02194

ABOUT THE AUTHOR

Award-winning author Nancy
Furstinger enjoys searching
for inspiring shapes in nature
as she hikes with her big
pooches. She is the author of
more than 100 books.

CONTENTS

FINDING YOUR RHYTHM

You come to music class with your brand-new drum. Try out different sounds by banging the drum with sticks, mallets, and your hands. Count out loud and play a steady beat. Or drum with wild rhythms.

Many drums are shaped like cylinders.

After music it's lunchtime. You packed a can of juice to drink. Did you notice how the shape of the drum matches the shape of the can? Both of these shapes are **cylinders**.

Many kinds of drinks come in cylinder-shaped cans.

Look at the chalk, markers, and paint pots. How many cylinders can you spot?

WHAT DOES A CYLINDER LOOK LIKE?

There are cylinders all over. Cylinders are not flat. They have three **dimensions**. Flat shapes, like a circle, have only two dimensions: length and width. Flat shapes can also be called plane shapes or 2-D shapes.

Shapes that have three dimensions are called **3-D** shapes. A cylinder has three dimensions we can measure: length, width, and height. 3-D shapes are also called solid shapes.

How do we tell if a shape is a cylinder? Look closely. A cylinder has two flat **faces**. These faces are two-dimensional flat **surfaces**.

The two flat, round faces, also called **bases**, are found on each end. If we trace around one of the cylinder's bases, we'll draw a circle!

A cylinder has both flat and curved surfaces. The third surface of a cylinder connects the two circle-shaped bases. It looks like a tube. This curved surface has straight sides. If we remove this face and lay it flat, it will form a rectangle.

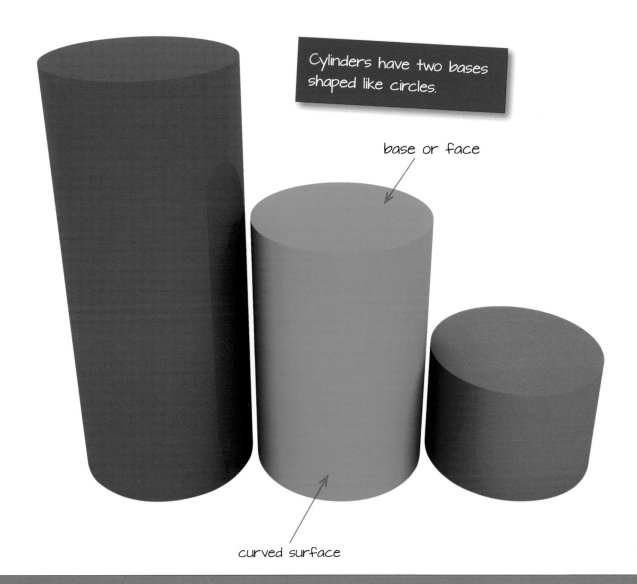

Cylinders have two bases shaped like circles.

base or face

curved surface

CYLINDERS AT THE STORE

Now you know how to spot a cylinder. You can see this 3-D shape everywhere in everyday objects.

Let's go shopping! Load up your shopping cart with healthy food. Get a bag of pasta tubes. Find your favorite strawberry yogurt. Toss in a big can of vegetable juice

Do you like any foods that come in cylinders?

and six more cans of alphabet soup. Don't forget rolls of paper towels. What other items can you find in cylinder-shaped containers?

Later you visit the craft store. You need supplies for art projects. Tiny glass bottles hold colorful beads. You can use the beads to fill a homemade kaleidoscope. Bright yarn winds around long spools. Colored pencils come packed in a plastic case. Add a glue stick and a can of spray paint to your cart. So many things have a cylinder shape!

CYLINDERS IN MACHINES

Cylinders also work hard inside different machines. Rolls of paper spin off of a machine onto a reel in a paper factory. A huge cylinder on a steamroller flattens new roads.

A steamroller rolls on a giant cylinder.

Smaller machines with this 3-D shape also help us work. A rolling pin makes it easy for us to roll out and flatten dough for pizza or cookies. A paint roller allows us to paint our bedroom walls our favorite color.

Have you ever painted anything?

Digging the Euro Tunnel

What did engineers use to dig the Euro Tunnel that connects Britain with France under the English Channel? They used tunnel-boring machines. These giant cylinders are as long as two football fields. The machines dug out 250 feet (76 m) of the tunnel each day. That is like digging out a 20-story building.

BUILDING WITH CYLINDERS

Cylinders form tall columns on buildings. These columns are called pillars. Some pillars help support the roof. Others decorate the building.

The US Capitol in Washington, DC, is famous for its columns. President George Washington chose the building's design. The original columns could not support the big iron dome on top of the Capitol. New columns were built. The old sandstone columns were set in a meadow with a reflecting pool. Now tourists can visit the National Capitol Columns.

The BMW Tower in Germany is shaped like four cylinders.

Quadruple Cylinders

A car inspired the BMW Tower in Germany. This skyscraper has four cylinder-shaped towers. They were designed to look like a car engine. Builders fitted together the glass and steel tower on the ground. Then they raised the towers 331 feet (101 m).

PIPES AND POLES

Other types of cylinders support or carry things. Pipes are shaped like cylinders. Copper, iron, and plastic pipes come in different widths. These pipes bring water and gases to our homes. Tall wood poles hold up power lines and cables. These wires carry electricity to our homes. They also bring us telephone service. The cylinder-shaped poles rise

Straws are like tiny pipes, and they are cylinders, too!

from 20 to 100 feet (6 to 30.5 m) tall.

Long, skinny poles help people swing up and over a high crossbar. Athletes compete in a track and field event called pole vaulting. Who can clear the greatest height? That person wins the gold medal. Whoever wants to beat the world record for pole vaulting will need to leap higher than 20 feet (6 m)!

A pole vaulter swings high into the air to vault over the crossbar.

Climb through the rope tunnel!

CYLINDERS AT PLAY

Cylinders can also be tons of fun. Most playgrounds have tunnel tubes that you can crawl, slide, or walk through. Some of these tunnels are made of rope. Use your hands to help you while the tunnel sways back and forth. When you reach the end of the tunnel, shoot down the slide!

You can make a fun tunnel playground for a pet mouse or gerbil. Save all of your empty paper towel cardboard tubes. Cut slits around the ends of the tubes to join them together. Your pet will have hours of fun playing in the tunnel system. As a bonus, you'll be recycling!

CYLINDERS IN NATURE

You can find cylinder shapes in nature. Many bamboo plants are shaped like cylinders. These plants grow quickly. Some bamboo can grow more than 3 feet (1 m) per day! In the desert, different types of cacti have cylinder shapes.

Bamboo stalks have a cylinder shape.

Worms' round bodies are similar to cylinders.

Watch out—they also have sharp spines!

If you take a nature walk, you might discover a log that forms a perfect cylinder. You might glimpse a snake slithering through the grass. Or you might discover worms wiggling beneath a rock. Both have cylinder-shaped bodies with no legs.

Be on the lookout for cylinders everywhere you go. It's amazing how many of these 3-D shapes you can find outside, inside, and all around!

HANDS-ON ACTIVITY: MAKE A DRUM

Make this cylinder-shaped drum. Then have fun drumming along to your favorite song!

Materials

- cylinder-shaped oatmeal container
- tape measure
- ruler
- pencil
- construction paper
- scissors
- glue stick
- yarn, glitter, stickers
- circle of waxed paper
- rubber band
- chopsticks or unsharpened pencils

Directions

1. Measure the dimensions of the oatmeal container using the tape measure.
2. Use the ruler and pencil to draw these measurements on the construction paper. Cut out the cylinder shape.
3. Glue the construction paper around the container.
4. Decorate your drum with yarn, glitter, and stickers.
5. Stretch the waxed paper circle over the open end of the drum. Hold it in place with the rubber band.
6. Then use chopsticks or unsharpened pencils as drumsticks. Drum on the waxed paper.

GLOSSARY

bases (BASE-es): Bases are the flat surfaces of a 3-D shape. A cylinder has two bases shaped like circles.

cylinders (SIL-un-ders): Cylinders are 3-D shapes with two flat circular bases and a curving round surface between them. Drinking straws and tin cans are two examples of cylinders.

dimensions (duh-MEN-shuns): Dimensions are the length, width, or height of an object. A cone's height is one of its dimensions.

faces (FASE-uhs): Faces are flat surfaces on a 3-D shape. A cylinder has two circular faces.

surfaces (SUR-fas-uhs): Surfaces are the flat or curved borders of a 3-D shape. A cylinder has two flat surfaces and one curved surface.

3-D (THREE-DEE): A 3-D shape has three dimensions, length, width, and height. A 3-D shape is not flat.

BOOKS

Cohen, Marina. *My Path to Math: 3-D Shapes*. New York: Crabtree
   Publishing Company, 2011.
Hoban, Tana. *Cubes, Cones, Cylinders, & Spheres*. New York: Greenwillow
   Books, 2000.

WEB SITES

Visit our Web site for links about Cylinders: *childsworld.com/links*

Note to Parents, Teachers, and Librarians:
We routinely verify our Web links to make sure they are safe and active sites.
So encourage your readers to check them out!

INDEX